The Wisdom of David Attenborough

Thoughts of a National Treasure

KENNY GORDON

Copyright © 2014 Kenny Gordon

All rights reserved.

ISBN: 1512268917
ISBN-13: 978-1512268911

DEDICATION

This book is dedicated to Sir David Attenborough who has inspired many with the rare views of nature he has brought to us and without whom this book would obviously not have been possible.

CONTENTS

1	Introduction	1
2	About Climate Change	3
3	About Himself	7
4	About Religion / God	15
5	About Animals	19
6	Philosophical and Thought-Provoking Quotes	29
7	Other Notable Quotes	39
8	A Brief Biography	49

DISCLAIMER

All quotes in this book have been carefully researched and collated as accurately as possible. However, the author apologises in the unlikely event of any inaccuracies.

1 INTRODUCTION

Sir David Attenborough is arguably one of the most respected people in modern Britain. His admirable respect for nature and the world in general is both inspiring and contagious.

Throughout my life I have been a fond follower of David to the point where I almost consider him a part of my extended family (although I have –unfortunately - never actually met him!). His genuine enthusiasm for the subjects he documents is always apparent and has undoubtedly contributed to his major success as a presenter and producer of some of the finest instances of British film-making.

As a personality, he is equally admirable and this has not gone unrecognised; aside from the numerous awards he has been presented with, he is renowned as a man of principles and ethics and, most of all, sincere integrity.

David has been quoted many times throughout the decades. Throughout this book I have brought together some of his finer known thoughts on a variety of issues.

KENNY GORDON

All of the quotes in this book are words spoken by the man himself.

2 ABOUT CLIMATE CHANGE

'There is no question that climate change is happening; the only arguable point is what part humans are playing in it.'

*

'Dealing with global warming doesn't mean we have all got to suddenly stop breathing. Dealing with global warming means that we have to stop waste, and if you travel for no reason whatsoever, that is a waste.'

*

'I would be absolutely astounded if population growth and industrialisation and all the stuff we are pumping into the atmosphere hadn't changed the climatic balance. Of course it has. There is no valid argument for denial.'

*

'The climate, the economic situation, rising birth rates; none of these things give me a lot of hope or reason to be optimistic.'

*

'We really need to kick the carbon habit and stop making our energy from burning things. Climate change is also really important. You can wreck one rainforest then move, drain one area of resources and move onto another, but climate change is global.'

*

'It's coming home to roost over the next 50 years or so. It's not just climate change; it's sheer space, places to grow food for this enormous horde. Either we limit our population growth or the natural world will do it for us, and the natural world is doing it for us right now.'

3 ABOUT HIMSELF

'It is vital that there is a narrator figure whom people believe. That's why I never do commercials. If I started saying that margarine was the same as motherhood, people would think I was a liar.'

*

'I can mention many moments that were unforgettable and revelatory. But the most single revelatory three minutes was the first time I put on scuba gear and dived on a coral reef. It's just the unbelievable fact that you can move in three dimensions.'

*

'I don't run a car, have never run a car. I could say that this is because I have this extremely tender environmentalist conscience, but the fact is I hate driving.'

*

About living in London:

'The climate suits me, and London has the greatest serious music that you can hear any day of the week in the world - you think it's going to be Vienna or Paris or somewhere, but if you go to Vienna or Paris and say, 'Let's hear some good music', there isn't any.'

*

'I suffer much less than many of my colleagues. I am perfectly able to go to Australia and film within three hours of arrival.'

*

'You know, it is a terrible thing to appear on television, because people think that you actually know what you're talking about.'

*

'Before the BBC, I joined the Navy in order to travel.'

*

'If I can make programmes when I'm 95, that would be fine. But I would think I'll have had enough by then.'

KENNY GORDON

*

'I'm luckier than my grandfather, who didn't move more than five miles from the village in which he was born.'

*

'If I can bicycle, I bicycle.'

*

'Well, I'm having a good time. Which makes me feel guilty too. How very English.'

*

'I just wish the world was twice as big and half of it was still unexplored.'

*

'I've been to Nepal, but I'd like to go to Tibet. It must be a wonderful place to go. I don't think there's anything there, but it would be a nice place to visit.'

*

'If I were beginning my career today, I don't think I would take the same direction. Television is at a crossroads at the moment. And although I am not up to date technologically, I suspect that somewhere out there people are conveying things about natural history by means other than television, and I think if I were beginning today, I'd be there.'

*

'I think a major element of jetlag is psychological. Nobody ever tells me what time it is at home.'

*

'I'm not in politics.'

*

'I had a huge advantage when I started 50 years ago - my job was secure. I didn't have to promote myself. These days there's far more pressure to make a mark, so the temptation is to make adventure television or personality shows. I hope the more didactic approach won't be lost.'

*

'I'm swanning round the world looking at the most fabulously interesting things. Such good fortune.'

*

'I don't approve of sunbathing, and it's bad for you.'

*

'I'm against this huge globalisation on the basis of economic advantage.'

*

'I am an ardent recycler. I would like to think that it works. I don't know whether it does or not.'

*

'I'm absolutely strict about it. When I land, I put my watch right, and I don't care what I feel like, I will go to bed at half past eleven. If that means going to bed early or late, that's what I live by. As soon as you get there, live by that time.'

*

'I'm not a propagandist, I'm not a polemicist; my primary interest is just looking at and trying to understand how animals work.'

4 ABOUT RELIGION / GOD

'I don't know [why we're here]. People sometimes say to me, 'Why don't you admit that the humming bird, the butterfly, the Bird of Paradise are proof of the wonderful things produced by Creation?' And I always say, well, when you say that, you've also got to think of a little boy sitting on a river bank, like here, in West Africa, that's got a little worm, a living organism, in his eye and boring through the eyeball and is slowly turning him blind. The Creator God that you believe in, presumably, also made that little worm. Now I personally find that difficult to accommodate...'

*

'As far as I'm concerned, if there is a supreme being then He chose organic evolution as a way of bringing into existence the natural world... which doesn't seem to me to be necessarily blasphemous at all.'

*

'I find it far more awesome, wonderful, that creation - our appearance in the world - should be the culmination, or at least one of the latest products of 3,000 Million years of organic evolution, than a kind of country trick, taking a rib out of a man's side in a trance.'

*

'The whole of science, and one is tempted to think the whole of the life of any thinking man, is trying to come to terms with the relationship between yourself and the natural world. Why are you here, and how do you fit in, and what's it all about.'

*

'To suggest that God specifically created a worm to torture small African children is blasphemy as far as I can see. The Archbishop of Canterbury doesn't believe that.'

*

'I often get letters, quite frequently, from people who say how they like the programmes a lot, but I never give credit to the almighty power that created nature.'

5 ABOUT ANIMALS

'People are not going to care about animal conservation unless they think that animals are worthwhile.'

*

'The question is, are we happy to suppose that our grandchildren may never be able to see an elephant except in a picture book?'

*

'The only way to save a rhinoceros is to save the environment in which it lives, because there's a mutual dependency between it and millions of other species of both animals and plants.'

*

'There are some four million different kinds of animals and plants in the world. Four million different solutions to the problems of staying alive.'

*

'Everywhere you look, on land or in the ocean, there are extraordinary examples of the lengths living things go to to stay alive.'

*

'Birds were flying from continent to continent long before we were. They reached the coldest place on Earth, Antarctica, long before we did. They can survive in the hottest of deserts. Some can remain on the wing for years at a time. They can girdle the globe. Now, we have taken over the earth and the sea and the sky, but with skill and care and knowledge, we can ensure that there is still a place on Earth for birds in all their beauty and variety. If we want to. And surely, we should.'

*

'I don't like rats, but there's not much else I don't like. The problem with rats is they have no fear of human beings, they're loaded with foul diseases, they would run the place given half the chance, and I've had them leap out of a lavatory while I've been sitting on it.'

*

'Reptiles and amphibians are sometimes seen as simple, primitive creatures. That's a long way from the truth. The fact that they are solar-powered means that their bodies require only 10% of the energy that mammals of a similar size require. At a time when we ourselves are becoming increasingly concerned about the way in which we get our energy from the environment and the wasteful way in which we use it, maybe there are things that we can learn from Life in Cold Blood.'

*

'Our planet may be home to 30 million different kinds of animals and plants. Each individual locked in its own life-long fight for survival.'

*

'Everyone likes birds. What wild creature is more accessible to our eyes and ears, as close to us and everyone in the world, as universal as a bird?'

*

'Birds are the most popular group in the animal kingdom. We feed them and tame them and think we know them. And yet they inhabit a world which is really rather mysterious.'

*

'I'm not an animal lover if that means you think things are nice if you can pat them, but I am intoxicated by animals.'

*

'I believe the Abominable Snowman may be real. I think there may be something in that.'

*

'Very few species have survived unchanged. There's one called lingula, which is a little shellfish, a little brachiopod about the size of my fingernail, that has survived for 500 million years, but it's survived by being unobtrusive and doing nothing, and you can't accuse human beings of that.'

*

'I like animals. I like natural history. The travel bit is not the important bit. The travel bit is what you have to do in order to go and look at animals.'

*

'What I am interested in with birds, just as I am with spiders or monkeys, is what they do and why they do it.'

*

'I'd like to see the giant squid. Nobody has ever seen one. I could tell you people who have spent thousands and thousands of pounds trying to see giant squid. I mean, we know they exist because we have seen dead ones. But I have never seen a living one. Nor has anybody else.'

*

'I've been bitten by a python. Not a very big one. I was being silly, saying: "Oh, it's not poisonous..." Then, wallop! But you have fear around animals.'

*

'If you watch animals objectively for any length of time, you're driven to the conclusion that their main aim in life is to pass on their genes to the next generation.'

*

'Birds are the most accomplished aeronauts the world has ever seen. They fly high and low, at great speed, and very slowly. And always with extraordinary precision and control.'

*

'Warm-bloodedness is one of the key factors that have enabled mammals to conquer the Earth, and to develop the most complex bodies in the animal kingdom.'

*

'Reptiles and amphibians are sometimes thought of as primitive, dull and dimwitted. In fact, of course, they can be lethally fast, spectacularly beautiful, surprisingly affectionate and very sophisticated.'

*

When he was asked whether knowing that animals are intelligent makes him want to be a vegetarian:

'If you understand about the natural world, we're a part of the system and you can't feed lions grass. But because we have the intelligence to choose… But we haven't got the gut to allow us to be totally vegetarian for a start. You can tell by the shape of our guts and the shape of our teeth that we evolved to be omnivores. We aren't carnivores like lions but neither are we elephants.'

6 PHILOSOPHICAL AND THOUGHT-PROVOKING QUOTES

'The most extraordinary thing about trying to piece together the missing links in the evolutionary story is that when you do find a missing link and put it in the story, you suddenly need all these other missing links to connect to the new discovery. The gaps and questions actually increase. It's extraordinary.'

*

'Three and a half million years separate the individual who left these footprints in the sands of Africa from the one who left them on the moon. A mere blink in the eye of evolution. Using his burgeoning intelligence, this most successful of all mammals has exploited the environment to produce food for an ever-increasing population. In spite of disasters when civilisations have over-reached themselves, that process has continued, indeed accelerated, even today. Now mankind is looking for food, not just on this planet but on others. Perhaps the time has now come to put that process into reverse. Instead of controlling the environment for the benefit of the population, perhaps it's time we control the population to allow the survival of the environment.'

*

'I mean, it is an extraordinary thing that a large proportion of your country and my country, of the citizens, never see a wild creature from dawn 'til dusk, unless it's a pigeon, which isn't really wild, which might come and settle near them.'

*

'Crying wolf is a real danger.'

*

'The fact is that no species has ever had such wholesale control over everything on earth, living or dead, as we now have. That lays upon us, whether we like it or not, an awesome responsibility. In our hands now lies not only our own future, but that of all other living creatures with whom we share the earth.'

*

'It seems to me that the natural world is the greatest source of excitement; the greatest source of visual beauty; the greatest source of intellectual interest. It is the greatest source of so much in life that makes life worth living.'

*

'The truth is: the natural world is changing. And we are totally dependent on that world. It provides our food, water and air. It is the most precious thing we have and we need to defend it.'

*

'If we and the rest of the backboned animals were to disappear overnight, the rest of the world would get on pretty well. But if they were to disappear, the land's ecosystems would collapse. The soil would lose its fertility. Many of the plants would no longer be pollinated. Lots of animals, amphibians, reptiles, birds, mammals would have nothing to eat. And our fields and pastures would be covered with dung and carrion. These small creatures are within a few inches of our feet, wherever we go on land – but often, they're disregarded. We would do very well to remember them.'

*

'It seems to me that the natural world is the greatest source of excitement; the greatest source of visual beauty; the greatest source of intellectual interest. It is the greatest source of so much in life that makes life worth living.'

*

'If my grandchildren were to look at me and say, 'You were aware species were disappearing and you did nothing, you said nothing', that I think is culpable. I don't know how much more they expect me to be doing, I'd better ask them.'

*

'People must feel that the natural world is important and valuable and beautiful and wonderful and an amazement and a pleasure.'

*

'Apart from anything else, I am designed by evolution, like we all are: if we see a little thing like that, big eyes, tiny nose, we go 'aaah'. That's what evolution does. We are programmed to do that. So to find babies the most amazing, isn't surprising, I don't think.'

*

'We keep putting on programmes about famine in Ethiopia; that's what's happening. Too many people there. They can't support themselves - and it's not an inhuman thing to say. It's the case. Until humanity manages to sort itself out and get a coordinated view about the planet it's going to get worse and worse.'

*

'The fundamental issue is the moral issue.'

*

'It's a moral question about whether we have the right to exterminate species.'

*

'Nature isn't positive in that way. It doesn't aim itself at you. It's not being unkind to you.'

*

'You can cry about death and very properly so, your own as well as anybody else's. But it's inevitable, so you'd better grapple with it and cope and be aware that not only is it inevitable, but it has always been inevitable, if you see what I mean.'

*

'You have to steer a course between not appalling people, but at the same time not misleading them.'

*

'It's extraordinary how self-obsessed human beings are. The things that people always go on about is, 'tell us about us', 'tell us about the first human being'. We are so self-obsessed with our own history. There is so much more out there than what connects to us.'

*

'If we [humans] disappeared overnight, the world would probably be better off.'

*

'The savage, rocky shores of Christmas Island, 200 miles south of Java, in the Indian Ocean. It's November, the moon is in its third quarter, and the sun is just setting. And in a few hours from now, on this very shore, a thousand million lives will be launched.'

*

'At a time when it's possible for thirty people to stand on the top of Everest in one day, Antarctica still remains a remote, lonely and desolate continent. A place where it's possible to see the splendours and immensities of the natural world at its most dramatic and, what's more, witness them almost exactly as they were, long, long before human beings ever arrived on the surface of this planet. Long may it remain so.'

KENNY GORDON

7 OTHER NOTABLE QUOTES

'Getting to places like Bangkok or Singapore was a hell of a sweat. But when you got there it was the back of beyond. It was just a series of small tin sheds.'

*

'All our environmental problems become easier to solve with fewer people and harder - and ultimately impossible to solve - with ever more people.'

*

'An understanding of the natural world and what's in it is a source of not only a great curiosity but great fulfilment.'

*

'We are a plague on the Earth.'

*

'Natural history is not about producing fables.'

*

'Being in touch with the natural world is crucial.'

*

About trees:

'Ever since we arrived on this planet as a species, we've cut them down, dug them up, burnt them and poisoned them. Today we're doing so on a greater scale than ever.'

*

'Vast movements of ocean and air currents bring dramatic change throughout the year.
And in a few special places, these seasonal changes create some of the greatest wildlife spectacles on earth.'

*

'Steve Irwin did wonderful conservation work but I

was uncomfortable about some of his stunts. Even if animals aren't aware that you are not treating them with respect, the viewers are.'

*

'In the old days... it was a basic, cardinal fact that producers didn't have opinions. When I was producing natural history programmes, I didn't use them as vehicles for my own opinion. They were factual programmes.'

*

'I don't think we are going to become extinct. We're very clever and extremely resourceful - and we will find ways of preserving ourselves, of that I'm sure. But whether our lives will be as rich as they are now is another question.'

*

'A hundred years ago, there were one and a half billion people on Earth. Now, over six billion crowd our fragile planet. But even so, there are still places barely touched by humanity.'

*

'I think we're lucky to be living when we are, because things are going to get worse.'

*

'Cameramen are among the most extraordinarily able and competent people I know. They have to have an insight into natural history that gives them a sixth sense of what the creature is going to do, so they can be ready to follow.'

*

'Television of course actually started in Britain in 1936, and it was a monopoly, and there was only one broadcaster and it operated on a license which is not the same as a government grant.'

*

'All we can hope for is that the thing is going to slowly and imperceptibly shift. All I can say is that 50 years ago there were no such thing as environmental policies.'

*

'London has fine museums; the British Library is one of the greatest library institutions in the world... It's got everything you want, really.'

*

'We are not overpopulated in an absolute sense; we've got the technology for 10 billion, probably 15 billion people, to live on this planet and live good lives. What we haven't done is developed our technology.'

*

'The more you go on, the less you need people standing between you and the animal and the camera waving their arms about.'

*

'The process of making natural history films is to try to prevent the animal knowing you are there, so you get glimpses of a non-human world, and that is a transporting thing.'

*

'It was regarded as a responsibility of the BBC to provide programs which have a broad spectrum of interest, and if there was a hole in that spectrum, then the BBC would fill it.'

*

'People talk about doom-laden scenarios happening in the future: they are happening in Africa now. You can see it perfectly clearly. Periodic famines are due to too many people living on land that can't sustain them.'

*

'Many individuals are doing what they can. But real success can only come if there is a change in our societies and in our economics and in our politics.'

*

'You can only get really unpopular decisions through if the electorate is convinced of the value of the environment. That's what natural history programmes should be for.'

*

'Trade is a proper and decent relationship, with dignity and respect on both sides.'

8 A BRIEF BIOGRAPHY

David was born in London on 8 May 1926. He is the younger brother of actor Lord Richard Attenborough.

He grew up in Leicester; his father, Frederick, was the principal of the University College there, and they lived on the campus.

During the war, his parents fostered two Jewish refugees from Europe.

He graduated from Cambridge University in 1947, having studied Natural Sciences.

Immediately after graduating he served 2 years National Service in the Royal Navy.

In 1950 he married Jane Oriel; their marriage lasted until her death in 1997. They had two children together, Robert and Susan.

In 1952 David joined the BBC, working as a producer. It was in 1954 when he first became a presenter, of the now famous series 'Zoo Quest'. Originally the show was planned to be presented by Jack Lester, curator of the zoo's reptile house; however, Lester was taken ill at short notice so David stepped in. This began his lengthy career as a documentary presenter.

David subsequently presented a variety of programmes, including political broadcasts, short stories, quizzes, gardening and religious programmes.

In 1964 he became Controller of the newly-launched BBC2, commissioning such programmes as Monty Python's Flying Circus, Call My Bluff, The Old Grey Whistle Test and The Money Programme.

In 1969 he was promoted to Director of Programmes for the BBC, giving him full responsibility for the output of both channels.

In 1972 his name was put forward for Director General of the BBC. David expressed little interest in the job. Shortly afterward he resigned from the BBC altogether to become a freelance documentary maker.

In 1973, he began filming the series 'Eastwards with Attenborough' with a crew from the Natural History Unit, shot in Indonesia. The series was a big success. Now back in presenting, David spent the following years as presenter of a number of different programmes, including children's series 'Fabulous Animals'.

It was in 1979 that his first 'Life' documentary aired. This was called 'Life on Earth' and took nature documentary filming to a completely new standard than ever before.

In 1985 David was awarded a knighthood and became Sir David Attenborough.

David continued his life series from then onwards. To date he has released 10 documentaries in the series, covering all main categories of species on the planet. He has also produced many other critically acclaimed documentaries, including Planet Earth, The Natural World and Frozen Planet.

Over the years, David has received honorary degrees from many universities across the world, and is patron or supporter of many charitable organisations, including acting as Patron of the World Land Trust, which buys rain forest and other lands to preserve them and the animals that live there.

With now over 60 years in broadcasting, he is generally considered a 'national treasure', yet reportedly does not like the term.

David remains the only person to have won BAFTAs for programmes in black & white, colour, HD and 3D.

ABOUT THE AUTHOR

Kenny Gordon is an avid nature enthusiast and freelance journalist. He is based in the South East of England but spends much of his time travelling the world. He is an animal lover and human rights campaigner.

CPSIA information can be obtained
at www.ICGtesting.com
Printed in the USA
LVHW031609071220
673555LV00045B/3751